MY TOWN

MY TOWN

WILLIAM WEGMAN

SCHOLASTIC INC.

NEW YORK
TORONTO
LONDON
AUCKLAND
SYDNEY
MEXICO CITY
NEW DELHI
HONG KONG

Chip's homework is to hand in a report on
a subject of his choosing. It's due tomorrow.

HOW ARE YOU DOING ON YOUR HOMEWORK, CHIP?

TEACHER McMILLAN

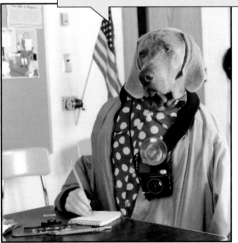

GOOD. I'M WORKING ON IT.

I HOPE SO! WHAT IS YOUR TOPIC GOING TO BE?

I HAVEN'T DECIDED YET. I'M ON MY WAY TO THE LIBRARY RIGHT NOW.

THE OTHER KIDS HAVE TURNED IN THEIR REPORTS ALREADY: NUCLEAR DISARMAMENT, GLOBAL WARMING, CHEMISTRY ON PARADE, ETC. . .

The library is a great place to get ideas.

COACH LOMBARDO

The coach always has good ideas. An inspiring pep talk is just what Chip needs.

What about talking to the art teacher? She's creative.

Do *you* have any ideas for Chip?

School's out, maybe Chip should go to town.

Ideas come from everywhere. There is no one way. Look in all directions.

PHOTO STORE OWNER DOYLE

Speaking of late, Chip should get zipping on that report, or he'll never deliver it.

Will Fire Chief Chundo get Chip fired up, kindle his tinder, flame his passion, hose his hesitations?

The situation is really quite alarming. Chip's homework is due **tomorrow!**

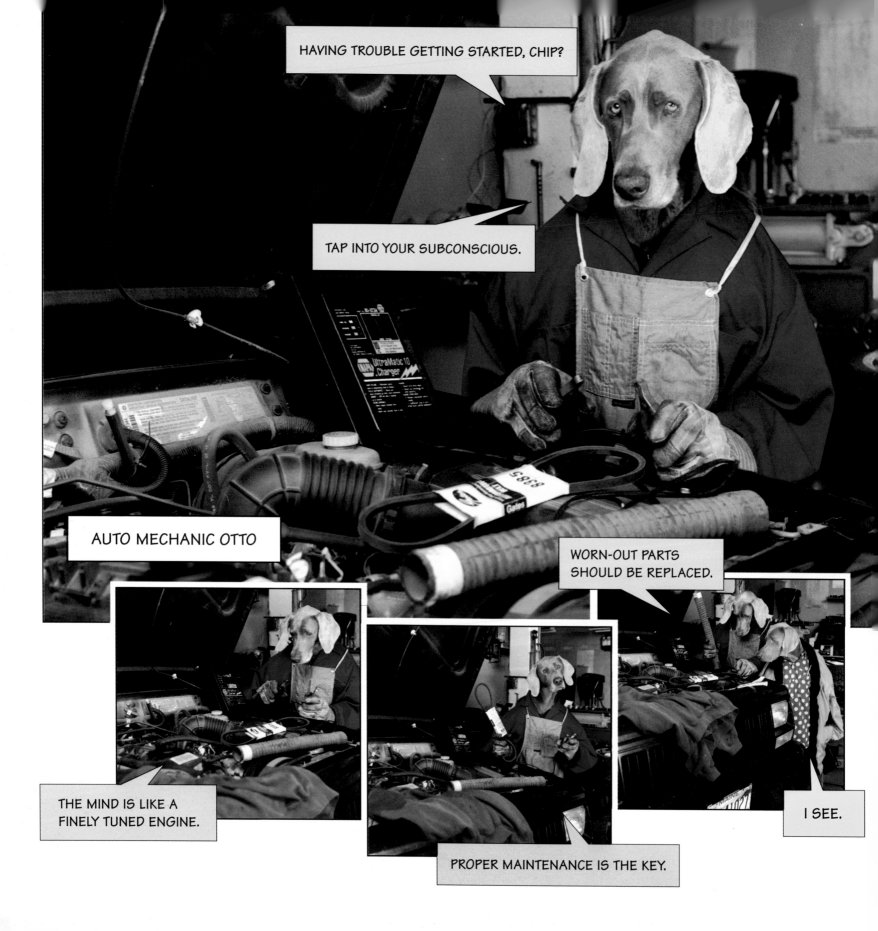

A visit to the auto repair shop and a quick check under the hood may help Chip.

ROTATE THE TIRES EVERY 5,000 MILES.

HMMM . . . RADIATOR HOSE OR FAN BELT?

HMMM . . .

KEEP THEM FILLED WITH AIR.

BUT DON'T OVERFILL THEM.

I'M UNDER TOO MUCH PRESSURE!

Perhaps getting his hair cut will make Chip
think better. Looking good is important.

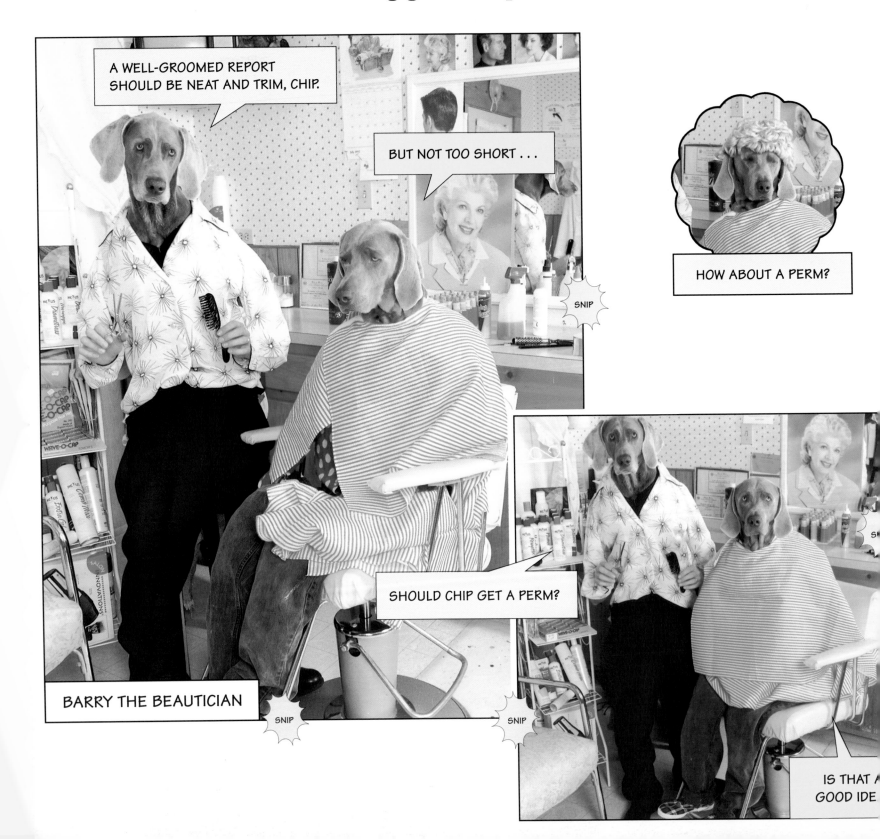

Chip should check out the supermarket
and shop around for ideas.

Maybe Chip should see a doctor.

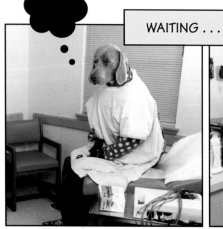

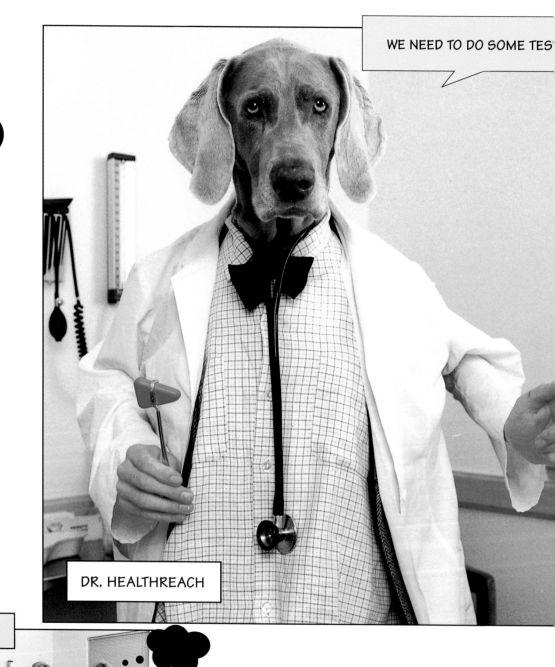

DR. HEALTHREACH

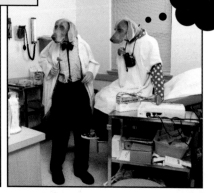

WAITING . . .

Is Chip okay?

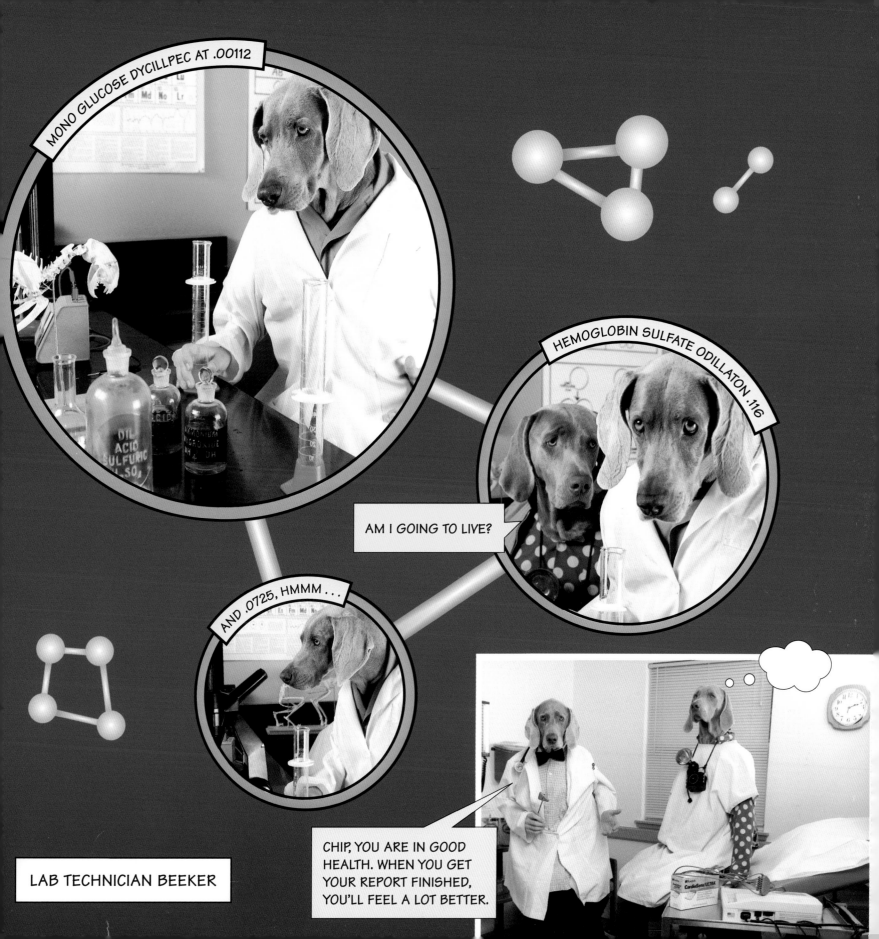

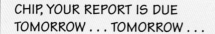

Chip is running out of time. Hey, wait a second . . .

Hey wait a second!

Teacher McMillan didn't say it had to be a *written* report (see page 5).

My Town

portraits
by Chip

A REPORT in pictures
a photo essay

DESIGN: DOYLE PARTNERS

THIS BOOK IS SET IN COURIER, CLARENDON, FALSTAFF, GROTESQUE, ROCKWELL, AND TEKTON

ACKNOWLEDGMENTS

WITH MANY THANKS TO THE PEOPLE OF THE TOWN OF RANGELEY: CHRIS AYLESWORTH; DAVIDSON'S GARAGE, WAYNE SEEMAN, OWNER; MEGGAN DAY; MADELEINE DE SINETY; FARMINGTON POST OFFICE; FRANKLIN SAVINGS BANK AND STAFF; AMY FREEMAN; DR. JAMES FREEMAN; FRENCHIE; HOLLY GARNER; SHEPARD GOLUB; SUSAN HAMILTON; REGGIE HAMMOND; SONJA JOHNSON; BARRY LIBBY, OWNER, THE BEAUTY BOUTIQUE; M&H CONSTRUCTION; LOONY MOOSE; JOEY, SHERYL, ASHLEY, BEN, ALEX, AND SHEVER MORTON; THE MAINE WARDEN SERVICE; ROGER AND PATSY PAGE; PERFECT PICTURES; POLLUTION CONTROL FACILITY AT CHICK HILL; RANGELEY FIRE DEPARTMENT, COMPANY NO. 1; RANGELEY IGA; RANGELEY INN AND STAFF; RANGELEY LAKES BUILDERS SUPPLY CO.; RANGELEY LAKES REGIONAL SCHOOL AND RANGELEY LAKES REGIONAL SCHOOL ART DEPARTMENT; RANGELEY POST OFFICE AND STAFF; RANGELEY REGION HEALTH CENTER; PRISCILLA AND BRIAN ST. LOUIS; HAROLD SCHAETZLE, FIRE CHIEF; CHARLES AND CAROL STEWARD; AND BOB AND TAMI WENTWORTH.

AND WITH THANKS FOR ALL THEIR HELP: STAN AND THEO BARTASH, ANDREA BEEMAN, CHRISTINE BURGIN, CRAIG CLARK, STEPHEN DOYLE, DOYLE PARTNERS, MATT GARTON, HYPERION, DAVE AND KERRY MCMILLAN, PACEWILDENSTEINMACGILL, THE PEEBLES FAMILY, HOWARD REEVES, TERRY ROZO, BRIDGET SHEILDS, AND KATHLEEN STERCK.

CHIP'S PHOTO ASSISTANTS; JASON BURCH, SKYE PEEBLES, JULIE HINDLEY, HEATHER MURRAY, PAM WEGMAN